Animal  Lives

CROCODILES AND ALLIGATORS

Sally Morgan

QED Publishing

QED

Copyright © QED Publishing 2006

First published in the UK in 2006 by
QED Publishing
A Quarto Group company
226 City Road
London EC1V 2TT

Reprinted in 2007

www.qed-publishing.co.uk

A Catalogue record for this book is available from the British Library.

ISBN 978 1 84538 699 3

Written by Sally Morgan
Designed by Jonathan Vipond
Editor Hannah Ray
Picture Researcher Joanne Forrest Smith

Publisher Steve Evans
Art Director Zeta Davies
Editorial Director Jean Coppendale

Printed and bound in China

Picture Credits

Key: t=top, b=bottom, l=left, r=right, c=centre, FC=front cover

Alamy/Bert de Ruiter 16bl, /Paul Wayne Wilson/PhotostockFile 27; **Corbis**/Jonathan Blair 10, 11, 13 /Brandon D Cole FC, /George McCarthy 5, /Joe McDonald 7t, /Martin Harvey/Gallo Images 12, 19tr, 30tl, /Peter Johnson 30br, /Stephanie Maze 1, /David A Northcott 30tr, /W Perry Conway 8–9, /Jeffrey L Rotman 28–29, /George Shelley 18–19; **FLPA**/Yva Momatiuk/ John Eastcott/Minden Pictures 20–21, /Mike Parry/Minden Pictures 16–17, /Fritz Polking 20tr, /Tui De Roy/Minden Pictures 7b, /Jurgen & Christine Sohns 24–25, /Eric Woods 14–15; **Getty Images**/Cousteau Society 4, /Ariadne Van Zandbergen 26; **NHPA**/E Hanumantha Rao 22, /Martin Wendler 15tr; **Photolibrary**/Michael Fogden; **Still Pictures** /Michael Fairchild 23.

Words in **bold** are explained in the Glossary on page 31.

Contents

Crocodiles and alligators

This Australian freshwater crocodile has extra-large scales along its back.

Crocodiles and alligators are fierce **predators** that live near water and are the largest of the world's **reptiles**. Reptiles are animals that have a skin that is covered with dry **scales**. Most reptiles, including crocodiles and alligators, lay eggs that have a leathery shell. Other reptiles include snakes, tortoises and lizards.

Appearance

Crocodiles and alligators look very similar. They both have long bodies and tails, which are covered in thick scales, and legs that stick out to the sides. Most crocodiles and alligators are between 1.8 and 3m in length, with the males being much larger than the females.

Both crocodiles and alligators, such as this American alligator, have a long snout with powerful jaws.

Types of crocodile and alligator

Gharials have very long, thin snouts with a pot-like tip.

There are 23 different **species**, or types, of crocodile and alligator. They are divided into three families: alligators, crocodiles and gharials.

The alligator family includes caimans and alligators, which range in size from 1 to 4m. The crocodile family includes the saltwater, Nile, New Guinea and American crocodiles. The gharial family includes just the gharial.

Telling the difference

The large fourth tooth in the lower jaw of an alligator fits into a socket in the upper jaw and is not visible when the alligator's mouth is closed. In crocodiles, this tooth is visible even when the crocodile's mouth is shut (see right).

Caimans are small and squat with extremely toothy grins.

Crocodile and alligator fact

Alligators have between 74 and 80 teeth. As the teeth wear down, they are replaced. An alligator can go through 2000 to 3000 teeth in a lifetime.

Where do you find crocodiles and alligators?

Crocodiles and alligators are found mostly in the **tropical** and subtropical parts of the world.

Alligators are found only in the south-eastern United States and in China, while caimans are found mostly in Central and South America. Crocodiles are found in many more places, including Florida, Central and South America, Africa, Pakistan, India, South-east Asia and northern Australia. The gharial is found in India, Nepal, Burma and Pakistan.

Crocodiles and alligators often spend the day lying in water to keep cool.

Areas where crocodiles
and alligators can be found

Wetland habitats

Crocodiles and alligators live in wetland **habitats**
such as tropical rainforests, swamps, along rivers,
in coastal **mangroves** and around ocean islands.

Although crocodiles and alligators can be found
in the same areas, they do not live closely
together. For example, in the Florida
Everglades, the American crocodile
is found near the sea where the
water is partly salty, while alligators
are found further inland where the
water is fresh.

Crocodile and alligator fact

Saltwater
crocodiles can swim
long distances. Some have
been found on remote islands
in the Pacific, more than
1300km from other
crocodiles.

9

Beginning life

Female crocodiles or alligators lay between 10 and 50 leathery eggs in a nest. Some species dig out a nest in the ground, but others make a mound by using their feet to gather up earth. Then they lay their eggs inside the mound. By laying her eggs either in the ground or in a mound of earth, the female makes sure the eggs stay warm.

Crocodile and
If the temperature in an alligator nest stays between 32°C and 33°C, most of the hatchlings will be male. If it is below 31°C or above 35°C, most are female.
alligator fact

This Nile crocodile is laying her eggs in a hole in the ground.

Guarding the nest

Most reptiles abandon their eggs once they have laid them, but female crocodiles and alligators guard their nests and attack any animal that comes too close. They only leave their nests to cool off in the shade or to have a quick dip in the water. In some species, the males stay close by too.

Despite the protection, not all the eggs hatch. Predators, such as monitor lizards and bears, raid the nests. Some nests are lost due to flooding, while others get too hot. Disease also kills some baby crocodiles or alligators while they are still in the egg.

These Nile crocodiles are guarding their eggs.

Hatching out

The eggs remain in the nest for between two and three months, depending on the species of crocodile or alligator. Just before hatching, the young crocodiles or alligators inside the eggs make lots of high-pitched sounds. These sounds tell the mother that they are about to hatch. She uses her legs to dig up the nest and help her hatchlings get to the surface. Often, she pushes her snout into the nest to find the eggs.

Hatchlings break out of their eggs by using a special egg tooth at the end of their jaw.

If baby crocodiles are in danger, the mother flips them into her mouth for protection.

Sometimes a hatchling can't break out of its egg. The mother takes the egg gently in her mouth and rolls it backwards and forwards on her tongue. This opens the shell and allows the hatchling to break free.

Once they have hatched, the mother picks up the hatchlings and carries them to water.

Growing up

The hatchlings stay together after they have hatched. During the day, they spread out to look for food, such as insects and small fish. Their mother is always nearby and she listens for their sounds.

The hatchlings usually stay with their mother for several months. Young American alligators stay close to their mother for up to two years. When they leave their mother, the young adults move out into the surrounding area.

Crocodile and alligator fact

Only around one per cent of young Australian saltwater crocodiles survive to reach adulthood.

Out of 35 American alligator hatchlings, only six will survive the first year.

Adult crocodiles do not have many enemies but some of the larger species of snake may attack an alligator or a caiman.

Larger is safer

Although young crocodiles and alligators are protected by their mothers, many are killed by predators such as snakes, lizards, birds of prey, hyenas and tigers. However, the number of crocodiles and alligators killed falls as they get larger. Once they reach a length of one metre, they are reasonably safe from predators.

Getting around

Crocodiles and alligators can move on land and in water. On land, they either walk slowly, dragging their tails along the ground, or they raise their bodies and tails up off the ground and walk on their toes. Using this 'high walk', they can also gallop surprisingly quickly, but only in a straight line and over a short distance as they soon tire.

Galloping crocodiles can reach speeds of up to 17km/h.

16

Crocodile and alligator fact

Young crocodiles and alligators can climb over obstacles several metres high.

Swimming

Crocodiles and alligators use their long muscular tail to propel their body through the water. When they swim, they hold their legs close to the sides of their body to create a streamlined shape that glides through the water.

Crocodiles steer and brake by sticking out their legs.

Underwater

Both alligators and crocodiles can float in the water with just their eyes and nostrils above the surface. They have a flap that closes off their mouths so they can breathe through their noses. They can dive and stay underwater for several minutes. Some have been known to stay underwater for as long as five hours.

17

Senses

Crocodiles and alligators have excellent senses which they use to find their **prey**. They have a special sense that enables them to detect movement in the water. Tiny **sensors** scattered over their face, especially around their mouth, can detect the tiniest **vibrations** caused by animals moving in and around the water.

Crocodile and alligator fact

Crocodiles have an extra reflective layer at the back of their eye so they can see more at night.

These lights on the surface of the water are reflections from the eyes of alligators.

Crocodile eyes

The eyes of these animals are covered by three eyelids. The third eyelid is **transparent** and covers the eye to protect it in the water. Crocodiles and alligators have vertical, cat-like **pupils** which get larger so they can see more in the dark. However, they cannot see much underwater.

Light passes through the black pupil into the eye of the crocodile.

Hunting

Crocodiles and alligators feed on a wide range of animals. Most lie in wait for their prey to pass close by. Some crocodiles and alligators float in the water, while others hide in the vegetation that lies at the water's edge.

This Nile crocodile has caught a gazelle.

Powerful jaws

Crocodiles and alligators grab their prey in their jaws and use their jaws to crush the body of the animal that they have caught. Usually the prey is drowned because the crocodile or alligator dives underwater with its catch.

Crocodile and alligator fact

Each year, crocodiles gather in the Mara River, in Africa, waiting to catch the wildebeests that cross it on their journey to find fresh grass.

Digestion

Crocodiles and alligators swallow their prey whole or break it up into large pieces. They do not have to eat every day because their bodies use up energy slowly. This means they can survive for several months without food, especially in cooler weather, when they are not so active.

Keeping cool

Reptiles are **ectothermic** animals, which means that their body temperature is similar to their surroundings. Crocodiles and alligators are only active when their bodies are warm, so in the morning they lie out in the sun to warm up. During the hottest hours of the day they either move into the shade or slip into the water to cool down.

Crocodiles and alligators open their mouths to help cool themselves down. This is called gaping.

Crocodiles and alligators lie in the shade during the hottest parts of the day

Overheating

After a period of activity, such as running after prey, the crocodile or alligator's body temperature rises and it often overheats. When this happens, it has to cool down by resting in the shade or lying in the water.

Living together

Crocodiles and alligators often meet up with other individuals of the same species to form groups. They **bask** in the sun together each day or gather at certain water holes. These groups are mostly females with one or two males. The individuals in these groups can recognize each other by the sounds they make.

Aggressive males

Male crocodiles and alligators don't like having many other males around so larger, older males tend to chase away the smaller males. As a result, younger males usually hang around the outside of a group. During the breeding season, the large males guard their territories and they do not let any other males approach the females.

This group of female alligators is basking in the sun. When they get too hot, they slip into the water.

Communication

Crocodiles and alligators make a wide range of sounds, including grunts, coughs, growls and **bellows**. They make a long, loud hiss as a warning before they are going to attack.

Some crocodiles and alligators slap their heads against the water to make a sound that travels a long way, while the gharial makes a popping sound. Many species produce bubbles when they are underwater and this creates sounds that others can hear.

This Nile crocodile inflates the pouch under its throat to make sounds.

Bellowing alligators

Male alligators bellow to attract a female and to warn off other males. When a male wants to bellow, he raises his head and tail out of water, waves his tail back and forth, puffs out his throat and shuts his mouth. Then he vibrates the air in his throat. This creates a vibration in the surrounding water that causes the ground and any other objects in or near the water to vibrate as well.

The vibrations created by this bellowing alligator are so strong, they make the water 'dance' up and down.

Crocodile and alligator fact

Glands under the chin of a crocodile or alligator release a special scent which they use to recognize each other.

Under threat

Crocodiles and alligators are hunted for their skin, which is used to make expensive shoes and handbags. In some places, so many crocodiles and alligators have been hunted that their numbers have fallen to very low levels.

Conservation successes

In 1971, the Australian saltwater crocodile had been hunted almost to extinction. Laws were passed to protect the crocodile, and now its numbers have returned to the levels that existed before hunting started. The number of crocodiles in Africa, South America and North America is increasing, too, because hunting is being controlled.

Farming

Crocodile and alligator farms help to protect crocodiles and alligators living in the wild. This is because the farmed animals provide skins and meat, leaving no reason to hunt wild animals.

In some places crocodiles and alligators are killed for their meat.

Crocodile and alligator fact

Before hunting was controlled in 1970, an estimated 10 million American alligators were killed for their skins.

Life cycle of a Nile crocodile

The female Nile crocodile is ready to breed when she is about 10 years old. She lays between 30 and 80 eggs in a nest and they hatch two to three months later. She cares for her young for up to two years.

The Nile crocodile lives to about 40 to 45 years old in the wild, but up to 80 years in captivity.

Full-grown crocodile

Glossary

bask to lie out in the sun

bellow make a roaring sound

ectothermic having a body temperature that is similar to that of the surrounding environment

extinct no longer in existence, disappeared completely

habitat the place in which an animal or plant lives

mangrove a group of tropical, evergreen trees that grow closely together in the salty water along a coastline

predator animal that hunts other animals

prey an animal that is hunted by a predator

pupil the dark spot in the middle of the eye

reptile an animal with dry skin covered in scales. Most reptiles, including crocodiles and alligators, lay eggs

scale a hard flake attached to the skin of a crocodile or alligator

sensor something that detects a stimulus such as a touch, a vibration or a smell

species a group of animals that look alike and can breed together to produce young

transparent clear, see-through

tropical the parts of the world near the Equator that are hot all year round

vibration a small to-and-fro movement

Index